fire pond

THE AGHA SHAHID ALI PRIZE IN POETRY

fire pond

Jessica Garratt

THE UNIVERSITY OF UTAH PRESS
Salt Lake City

PRIZE IN POETRY

The Agha Shahid Ali Prize in Poetry

Series Editor: Katharine Coles
Advisory Editor: Peter Covino

 The Defiance House Man colophon is a registered trademark
of the University of Utah Press. It is based upon a four-foot-tall,
Ancient Puebloan pictograph (late PIII) near Glen Canyon, Utah.

13   12   11   10   09   1   2   3   4   5

Library of Congress Cataloging-in-Publication Data
Garratt, Jessica, 1977-
Fire Pond / Jessica Garratt.
        p. cm.—"Winner of the 2008 Agha Shahid Ali prize in poetry."
ISBN 978-0-87480-953-4 (pbk. : alk. paper)
I. Title.
PS3607 .A766F57 2009
811'.6—dc22   2009006292

Cover art: *Sanctum* by Will Barnet. 1976, oil on canvas, 42 ½ x 54 ½ inches. Courtesy
of Babcock Galleries. Art © Will Barnet/Licensed by VAGA, New York, NY.

For my family

Contents

Abstract   *1*

I.

Cogito   ✦   *5*

Without   ✦   *8*

Answer This   ✦   *10*

Foundation   ✦   *12*

The State of Things   ✦   *15*

En Route   ✦   *16*

Transmission   ✦   *18*

Neighborhood   ✦   *19*

Mirador   ✦   *20*

Home after a weekend with old friends   ✦   *23*

Permanence   ✦   *25*

Leaving Sykesville   ✦   *27*

Climate of Refrain   ✦   *29*

Rotation   ✦   *30*

Farewell!   ✦   *32*

II.

Fire Pond   ✦   *35*

III.

Woman drives past, crying   •   *47*

Infidelity   •   *48*

First Flight   •   *50*

Elegy   •   *52*

The End of Things   •   *54*

True North   •   *55*

Self-Preservation Ode   •   *56*

Epilogue   •   *58*

Pilgrim   •   *59*

Things said (me & others, dreams & waking, yesterday
    & years ago): An Exorcism   •   *61*

Expression   •   *63*

Brooklyn, February   •   *67*

Fascicle   •   *73*

Notes   •   *77*

Acknowledgments   •   *79*

Abstract

Many are alone.
        That's the specific and the universal
                truth. Specifically, I feel alone
on & in the face
        of the universe,
                though I might not
if that stingy largesse might contract
        into a face & a smile & a body
                like the last one, dear
god; the soul of one
        tucked away in one
                whose face is still smooth
with infinity. How might I love
        anyone less? How can I be more
                specific than I am? Outside
a gray steel football turns
        wise as a clock
                on the back of an idling truck.
Upside-down, CONCRETE
        appears, disappears, reappears
                in big red painted letters, turning
for someone I can't see
        on the other side of the truck, only
                right side up.

I.

Cogito

The maple outside my window
shakes its big yellow fever at me,
a spotlight in the wind. I'm in bed
reading *First Meditation, Concerning
Things That Can Be Doubted,*
from a textbook with a neon *Used* sticker
glued to its spine. My throat
is lemon-peel sore, but luckily, like Descartes,
I'm disturbed by no passions
these days. I'm free
in my peaceful solitude
to draw the quilts up to my chin
and think. Elsewhere, a wail
of tires, the soft crush of metal
on metal on an unseen street
as fenders furrow like eyebrows.
The storm windows rattle.
Descartes is seated by the fire
in his winter dressing gown, the paper
in his hands bearing the reason
for doubting every belief in his senses'
deceptive creed. For, what if,
right now, he was only his own
dream, haunting the attic
of his true body (naked, fast asleep
between the bedsheets in another room),
the fire only a painted fire,
drying on the twin, fluttering canvases
of his eyelids? Descartes is locked
in a vise, a bracket in black
ballpoint pen. A boy named Adam
owned this book before I did. He paid

his money, read some
of what he was told to read,
then thrust it back into the world
when the semester was finished
henpecking him. Adam didn't like
Descartes. He scrawled insults, all caps,
in the white oblivion of the margins.
The delicate, imagined hem
of Descartes' dressing gown did nothing
to touch him. Instead, he wrote *DICK*
beside the fire scene, the letters large and hard
as the clang of a grate, slammed shut
in a silent room. I can almost see
the tough grudge of his shoulders,
fending off the intrusion of books,
which burden him with the suggestion
that he might not be everything,
or enough. What was this book (dead
on the shelves of cinderblocks
and two-by-fours lining the blank edge
of his room) compared to what he had suffered
in the space of a single day,
when he got dumped, maybe, and walked around
like a long, thin papercut
before it bleeds? Descartes drew a diagram
of pain, to show how it was separate
from the mind: a resigned cherub of a man,
one toe dipped in the furled cabbage
of a fire, parting the skin, opening a hollow
extension cord, hooked up to the brain,
for the *animal spirit* to flow through
and inflate the muscle, inviting the leg
to withdraw. Adam withdrew.
But his dreams stuck around like brick
tenements, blocking the view, the sun, his mind

pale, hacking up images
of people and places, gluing them
to 1989, to yesterday, to never,
with a hot, tacky shame that wouldn't dry evenly,
or hold. He woke each morning with half
an erection, aimed at no one, no place
in particular, the constellation of acne scars
on his roommate's back a sign
that nothing mattered, the closed curtains
a shade of green that said the same,
as dim, beer-thin watts of winter light
nudged them, the storm windows rattling.
Descartes recorded only the three
consecutive dreams (plotted clearly
as points on a plane, arcing upward)
that drove him to unearth the *foundation
of the wonderful science*. He was twenty-three
at the time, and had to believe
in a divine destiny, since his father called René
his one disappointment in life, a *son so ridiculous
as to have himself bound in calfskin!*
So the son could do nothing
but prove God—a God that made the real
him. His parents were responsible
for his body (that modest, restless curtain
concealing the open window
of his true, immaterial self). There was nothing
he could do about that—except doubt
everything but what he thought
they could not touch or ruin; nothing to do
except make them not matter—as perhaps Adam
made Descartes not matter, made everything matter
as little as possible, in order to ignore
the *other* edge of the knife laid down inside him:
hopeful, threatening to try something new.

Without

Be—and yet know the great void where all things begin,
the infinite source of your own most intense vibration,
so that, this once, you may give it your perfect assent.

—Rainer Maria Rilke

As if the reflected future of a stone in air over water, the summer's loose
collection of rings—its distraction of swimming pools and waiting

tables, errands listed and run, mostly for the sake of not being the one
caught standing still and alone, the music stopped—suddenly

assembled themselves and telescoped down to a single point, a single
moment, intimate, not mine: The drowning of a man who was once a boy

at my college, a boy I didn't even know, only knew him to see him—
tall, acne-scarred, strolling the paths of campus in too-big jeans, ears muffed

by headphones, hair slicked and impenetrable to the seasons'
small invasions. I wonder now if the moment of his death didn't also

travel those paths, a weightless freckle in his vision he barely noticed
but saw everything through. Who can say? It's puckered shut now

to all but he who has been licked clean of speech, clean of the relief
of retelling. What happens when the two finally have it out? When animal
    panic breathes

down the pale neck of consciousness and isn't forced back
to its corner by the fluke of regained footing, or an outstretched hand,

when the *puh* of relief is never allowed to surface? No sob, no laugh,
just the tough panic of flesh and muscle, staying tough, letting nothing

pass, the brain flapping open and shut according to some new will, dilating
    wildly
as a pupil in the impossible light of a dream. What if, in our last moments,
    nothing

but the water adjusts: if the mind *doesn't* take hold of the body's hand
as it dies—if the body dies alone, desperate, only a body, and the mind

darkens, a scrap of torn sail, tossed on the waves? As the final
breath dislodged from his lungs, what if he didn't know

it was his final breath? He was still just trying to breathe:
as an animal might, to the last, without thought or witness,

without groping inward toward that cold, intimate stone.

Answer This

Quick: It's your last night as you.
What, then, must be written before tomorrow

erases for good the chance you've been forfeiting all summer
to say something that matters to someone,

if only you? First thought: *My family, my friends, the homage to them*
I've never written. (Nothing happens.)

What about the one I've lost, but have loved for years
out of habit, or else much more? (Doesn't stick.)

Beneath this flash of forced connections—
between the brain and the quick diorama it reduces

the world to, under pressure—I notice,
in shifting, shallow light, a scene like a vista

opening, rooted loose as seaweed in last week:
Independence Day. Nothing to do. Went to a movie alone.

Driving home, still soaked in the movie's humid pathos,
I saw that storm clouds had gathered low, the small square

of downtown relieved now of cars, the shop windows
vacant, absorbed. Pressed beneath the clouds

churning in frothy slow motion, the town appeared
flimsy, made of cardboard, half-sunk

back into ground, a shipwreck of a town, hardly recalled,
with only an unconscious life, or a life inside

someone else's unconscious,
shuffling incongruously, imagistically beneath the hoopla

of fireworks and barbecues, sweaty beers palmed in dreaming hands
crowned by watches rescued just in time

from the hold of a shop now sinking away
from what little impression it made on the air, on the minds

of the departed ones. I was so glad to be alone
in this inside-out version of where I had lived, where the sky

had once tucked neat as hospital-corners beneath the edge
of town, behind the noon dropcloth of gossip.

All that lifted now, a circus pulling up stakes, its many eyes turned
distantly toward the next arrival on its itinerary.

I was so full, suddenly, with that particular sodden joy
of being left behind, I thought something might actually

happen. I knew better, but was glad
to not know it so well that I couldn't hope this time

would be different. It wasn't. That's okay.
I knew, even without the high point overlooking a windy expanse

of sea or prairie I now found myself
craving, that this feeling would feed whatever good

came of my life, and went to sleep that night
amid the pop and soar of late, illegal fireworks,

launched from small yards I couldn't see.

Foundation

I began to think of my body
        the same nervous way I think of the world
                these spring afternoons, when everything is so
jubilant, it seems the day is exactly
        what it would be if it could choose
                anything. Trees moving, slurred patches
of light, birds' throats strung with a wilderness
        of joy. This can't possibly
                be the whole story. I don't even understand,
though I can imagine, in my own way
        of imagining, slow poison, alloyed with hard
                violence, a thick atmosphere
the world cathedrals into, tries
        to grow through, trying to continue
                being itself, with spring days that still
have that effortless feel, that show
        without straining against the black, heavy cloth
                we sometimes have to strain
to see, through so much green. The body too
        keeps reeling through its actions, even
                after something's gone wrong. You might not realize
some equal but opposite force has begun
        to build, until your body begins to slow
                against its pressure. In the mirror, my body
looks like itself to me, and will, I imagine, while I'm
        still in it, no matter what may be tainting its waters,
                soaking up, then draining its health, cell
by cell, until it's not about imagination
        anymore, or the sets of images the mind
                applies. Until it's nothing to do

with the mind, but with *reality*.
        So I tried to peer hard
                through what seemed the deceptive surface,
down into what I perceived
        as the depths—the truth—the thing I could be
                missing. What I couldn't see, I felt—
little twigs snapping in a thicket, deep inside
        some woods. That's how the sensations began.
                But the more attention I gave, the more
they flared, little campfires growing, trying
        to light the entire sky. A pain
                in my abdomen, a headache, a numb tingling
down my right side, the garish look of the veins
        in the palms of my hands when I woke up
                in the middle of the night, my heart
a thing trapped inside a thing, shortening
        my breath, washing up little waves
                of lightness behind my eyes so I couldn't see
anything, except that I might die, at any moment, no matter what
        the doctors said, their tests
                skimming the surfaces of me, while
the real threat lurked far deeper, and would never
        risk itself for such paltry bait, would rather
                wait—take my whole life
at once. I had to be vigilant, suspect everything,
        even the man I lived with at the time, even he
                was out to get me, to end my life, noticing other
women as he did. I know. I had a lookout.
        I perched high above what could be called
                the *actual events*—a meal at a restaurant, a walk into town,
drinks—and searched constantly for a flash
        of subtext, a sign that something was amiss,
                that I was right to keep watch—it was necessary.

Not being desired—no, not
        being wanted—seemed almost as dire
                as blood clots or tumors. I was afraid
of everything. No, that's wrong. I had a craving
        for safety. Something in me sank
                each time I saw a mother swinging her child
on the playground nearby, or a couple
        laughing in that lifelong way.
                TV shows were square, wrapped packages
sent to me from the distant zip code of an ordered city
        that would never have me. The room
                flashed blue, and my heart drifted like bits of lint
through the light, not connected to anything,
        not even held together, while everyone else
                had the future in their eyes, lit like a road
they knew how to drive, a highway bright
        with unquestioned speed, no thoughts
                about how low were the concrete walls
lining the narrow overpass, no thoughts
        about what happens if you're forced suddenly
                from your lane.
The future didn't belong to me.
        It was sealed off, the way that man was
                in those terrible seconds when I'd realize
he was a world all to himself. His existence
        had nothing to do with me. How could I accept
                such disregard for the space I took up?
I might disappear with so little to hold me.
        I wanted someone to look at me
                and never stop. Someone to say,
I'll notice, I'll fix it
        if anything goes wrong.

The state of things

She is suddenly convinced
(before a sturdier thought
can push to the head
of the line) that she knows the answer, that if only
she had plants
(the room for an instant grows
green and comforting, vines curl down the walls
like pretty hair caught with leaves)
if only there were plants
everywhere, never
thinking, but breathing
the same light, needing
to be fed, hanging from the ceiling
as though it were a small sky, cupped close
to their sinless leaves—
maybe then
(the room empties; the walls
pale; the furniture
is sewn with dead leaves)
safety and health would reach for her too, hold her
as a mother would—as though
it might never be otherwise.

En Route

"Trust me, airplanes *want* to stay in the air,"
says the man who fills the seat next to me
with his physique, a fluid sort
of flotation device, charming, he thinks,
my hissing nerves from their basket.
The huge engine of blue serenity we see, hear
snoring, cool cheek pressed to our windows,
is not there. Instead, we hang among a salad
in the making, the blue vegetable world
being chopped and diced and tossed
as only the invisible can, while
the man's theorem chimes the chime
of a grandfather clock—with the benefit, I mean,
of never sounding wrong. A sound that sounds
as though it's torn from the cosmic palate.
I've always admired statements unedited
by any timid echo clouding up
from the heels of an inner waffler—
and up here, sound isn't encouraged
to travel. What alien loveliness
to hand something to the world, and know the world
won't shove it back; to be certain your guts are gutsier
than its, or else, more simply, to believe
a Platonic marriage exists
between your mind and the principles so vigorously underlined
in the world's dog-eared manual.
But can you blame a certain kind
of stomach, home to a crowd of butterflies—or
are they sheep?—a crowd of sheep
doddering harder and harder into the idea of "herd"—
for hunkering deeper, and lurching

when such a dare, hanging operatically in the rafters,
is put to the wolves of circumstance?
Surely the plane can't pass up such temptation
to let go of the air
a retired engineer breathed long ago
into the arctic lines and openings
of its blueprint. Surely it's too efficient
to be blessed or doomed
to want more than anything
the very thing you're good for. To always believe
in the circle, it's exhausting,
the thrice-checked fuel, the round-trip, ironclad halves
of expectation and delivery. Failure is the natural response
to such innocence and completion.
How strange *all* the planes haven't fallen.

Transmission

Last night, lodged in my room,
     loose as a screw
in one board
     of a larger structure,
the dark was possessed

by the same dull static
     that had come alive
in my arm, dim sparks pricking
     the empty space
where blood had coursed easily
     before the weight of my body

restricted its flow
     to a keyhole. Thoughts came
incidentally, tinsely
     wrappers torn off and discarded,
trashing up the dark
     with throw-away noise.

This is how the Earth must look
     from space—obscured
by its own doing, in a hairshirt
     of sound, light, trash, spinning
to avoid spinning's opposite.
     No.

I've seen, of course, the serene reels
     from the satellite's oracle eye:
Earth's "spin" a mulling over
     of motion, its revolution
imperceptible.

Neighborhood

The young men in their bright padded uniforms
could—except for their coach with his muddy
tattoo, his shades—they could be young men
of any age, any day this century. I have no idea

of the thoughts that churn without center, inside
their close haircuts; or what climate, what private
weather has clothed the slow lengthening

of their bones. But, from here, from this
window—does it matter?

The sky is sufficiently blank.

You could never tell by looking
whether it meant to resemble a high marble ceiling, a pall,
or just someone's painting of clouds before rain.

You could never tell if it was a lid, closed
on peace or on war.
Or if an eye lay behind it, alive
in the dark, knowing
                              the difference.

Meanwhile, the young men practice.

Mirador

I'm so used to this view
        producing what's lithe, contained
                by leaf-shape or squirrel-form, fluster
of wings—motion with a shine
        of metabolism, a clear enamel
                waxing the *fixed & dead*
matter beneath it—that this, this
        lolling grotesquerie, this shaped
                undulation of mass and fur
balanced behind a quivering screen
        of leaves (flash of thick neck,
                masked face) ousts me
from internal drift.
        A dampness has been darkening all day
                in the upper reaches of the maple.
From my bleached state among the bedsheets,
        the lime and jade tense shifts
                of the leaves
around that body, those small dark eyes,
        shame me into view. Something
                my mother told me just yesterday
about our muscles, our six-hundred
        muscles, eager as mice
                in the walls, or empty traps
in a wilderness, poised to gnash
        their aluminum teeth, and most of us
                setting only fifty or so free
our whole lives. This is the root
        of arthritis, plus other difficulties,
                according to the theories she's learning.

Those fifty muscles are overworked,
        grown sore, then almost numb
                inside the condition of pain,
while the others lie about, pale
        with leisure: *To a diseased degree*
                disconnected from motion & action,
says Coleridge, sulking
        over his failed imagination.
                What's not in motion is basically dead,
says my mother.
        If my muscles were metaphysical
                I wonder how my life would move.
Which reflexes do I over use? Which shrink
        toward the grave too early, having learned
                morbid helplessness?
Has the growing dark outside
        made mirrors of the windows,
                so the air inside is a reflected pressure, stale,
more barroom than soul?
        Last night my friend said on the phone
                he's been thinking too much about death.
What if some evening he has to see his wife
        alive one second, gone the next?
                What will he tell her
just before she leaves, when no comfort is left
        in words? His two-year-old daughter,
                how will he tell her
that she too will go someday?
        This is why we shouldn't have given up God,
                he said. I finished his sentence
internally: *so there'd always be something left*
        to say. So we wouldn't have to feel
                still, powerless, silent,

in the face of someone we've failed
        to love forever, and find
                our own death there, a sentence
trailing off, unfinishable
        thought. I barely remember
                the little girl, same age
as me, who didn't come back
        from the Eastern Shore, who slipped
                beneath the bay's smooth blade for good.
Her death didn't come with words,
        but salty green pictures of water, rocks, parents
                on the shore, the voice of the sun
in my mother's throat as she told me.
        The girl's wet hair.
                The space where she was, then wasn't.
Now I imagine her six-hundred muscles,
        tiny, alive, straining toward what
                she barely knew yet, with complete loyalty.
We must not go on this way, friend,
        knowing what we know about things.
                Why not lift all our six-hundred muscles
to joy? We can. *We receive but what we give.*
        The raccoon begins to climb down.

Home after a weekend with old friends

Who knows what will happen to me

if I stretch out beneath these bleached marine fossils
of last week's sleep,

or sit still long enough, with a book, in this atrophied muscle
of a chair?

Thursday's hasty arrangement
of old poems in a new order
retires on my desk, a fan of frozen tail feathers.
It makes my jaw ache, the way an old candid snapshot can:

force your lonely, park-bench gaze
on the lively gloss of its countenance, and the expression
within the expression

falters, tries to turn
back to the coliseum of gossip, being built beyond the precipice
of its shoulder. It's hard to tell sometimes

if this world we inhabit
is a sacred convent of souls, or merely a convention
of nuns, dressed in plain clothes, driving cars
between prayers. Never mind

these rooms' melodrama of spells and swoons,
the walls and furniture turning pale on a dime
beneath their ruin,
beneath the fine frost of apocalypse ash

they make believe—this apartment
still won't get what it wants from me.

I light a candle, set it in the window, so someone
else can burn
with rootless, night-dwelling envy

as she looks up from the dark street, wishing to stop
herself from wanting
to pass through that keyhole of flame.

Permanence

In Iowa, it is late afternoon, going on evening. It's early autumn,
    and if it were years ago, I might be walking back to my dorm
along streets with enormous changing trees, houses

      with families inside them, thoughts of dinner warming
their windows. That yellow light paled my heart, dried it up
    like a piece of fruit because of how much I missed myself

inside it. In the dorm, light was different. It fell from every direction
    at once, sopping up the dark completely, uniformly,
as if the future had sat down upon us—bleak, durable,

      sordidly aloof—and I had no idea how to get out
from under it, or act like myself beneath it. So I spent long afternoons
    in the library that felt permanent, the sunken hours

till dinner sewn tightly into the blank fields outside by the pulse
    of quiet glances over the tops of books—books
in which I recognized smudged shapes that had roughed the surface

      of my heart for years, encased now in the elegance of form.
Those readings braided themselves with my lonely obsessions, home
    being farther than it had ever been, the feeling that time had washed me

onto a strange, shoreless land, then slipped away again, depositing me
    among hours that didn't leave, but hovered, at times like bees
or relentless light at noon, at times like moonlight, sloshed

through the trees, over the cold grid of the fire escape. I held still. I listened.
     Sometimes, leaving the evening's vacancy
of soccer fields for the warm ringing angles of the dining hall,

     I felt I was entering a great heart, swollen to its rafters
with solitude, lined all over with bright, ecstatic nerves,
     the glint of poised cutlery.

Leaving Sykesville

There's never an ill fit. Nothing snags or catches
in the sleeve of its own existence. Through

mountains and crops I drove, each town a tarred knot
of freeway, clotted with food, flores-

cence, gasoline, A/C. From one edge, out
to the middle, the Midwest. As if a map

long anchored by its two doting oceans
were suddenly let go, and scrolled inward

between tidal waves—that's how it was
to leave again that old Maryland landscape

so comfortably married to its own features
it began to turn inward, and run like water-

color, or subject matter, beneath
the physical lines—the ceremony

of being leaving itself behind
for the river of eternal forms

collecting downhill of my life. But not really.
Objects, landscapes, walls we pose to dam

the slosh of space—they are what they are, don't pace
in or out the doorways of themselves.

Each one is a perfectly packed trunk:
no gaps, no wasted space. My departure

was no more departure than the act my hand
rehearses right now, wading through an apparent swell

of emptiness, mild heat rising from what appears
an ordained path, cleared for sake of reach

and mug. But never for a moment
does it tear a margin, or knock a chance

clearing in the evening element
of existence; never is it not

a perfect fit, despite our experience
of friction, striking a spark among the dry

grasses that live behind our skin, nerving an interior
expanse we can only know, or say exists.

Climate of Refrain

From down here the hill steeps up
not to the blade peak of a vanishing
point, but to a dull line staffed
by trees. And yet the hill must lumber
toward me, a stone wall being inclined
to dam the crash of earth's trajectory, as if
by necessity, though with no real effort
I can see. Perhaps the crook
and lean of individual stones
speak of strain, interrupted as they are
by moss, that willing waylayer of any
measure not its own. Still, nothing
a little upkeep won't fix. Wilderness, this
is not. I sit out back of a rented home,
steeped in the windy husk
of leaves. Squirrels leap and swing
overhead, as though squirreling
were the only real business
these days. Each time a local
gust drops by, some wooden chimes
I never bought pock the air
with the sound of closed mouths
bumping into each other.

Rotation

When a day is bright, when we can see everything
nicely, because some energy moves

behind and inside the air, wholly separate
from it—an energy that travels quite quickly but appears

still, and unscientific, as lives do, as does
one moment inside a mind, full and muted

as a lake—when this thing called light looses
upon half the earth, it is for a reason: the earth

is suspended in a great clearing, having rooted there, and grown
over a very large number of moments,

each one thick as the meaning that swims, more
ancient than turtles, beneath the word *now*—

and when this earth turns one of its faces
in one direction, and someone driving to work squints, curses

the light, it is because, rising up from behind the highway,
between the trees where birds come alive—singing,

a bright pattern crossing the stark inner walls
of their biology—is a star.

The woman drives slowly into a star, half swallowed
by exhaustion, but relieved to at last be rescued

by day—at last she is no longer crushed by the pressure
to sleep (sleep!) through the unignorable stillness

of the house, of everything but the trees and the clock,
and herself, wandering through dark painted halls, down

creaking stairs, with fresh concerns for the sturdiness
of her mind—for she wondered last night, stuck inside

the confusion of a single moment, revolving and divided, somehow,
from all other moments—she wondered about rooms, what a house is, what

one is for. She thought (though by morning she would
forget) that no matter which way the earth is turned, we are still stuck

in moments like this one, full and muted as a room with someone
inside it, as the meaning that sifts like dirt under floorboards, like

one instant of pain, like her whole childhood, toted around
inside, an entire life beneath the word *now*.

Farewell!

Out walking last evening (past stables, the fireflies
low along the tree line, a brief warm gust
quickening some current that repeated
in me), I watched as I climbed over
a blurred version of the fence, and broke
into a wild tear toward the horses
dining solemnly together on the hill.
And, at first, as just after a dream, it wasn't clear
which was *me*—the one who ran, a cry dislodged
like red magician's silk from her throat,
or the one who continued to trace with her steps
the simple intention of the fence, economical
inside her life. It wasn't clear who was who
until one let go—the way a child lets go
of balloon after balloon, across years,
and only with practice is able to watch
that bright shape float away
and not feel herself go with it.

II.

Fire Pond

(Peterborough, NH)

I

Lately, there's never not a reason good
enough to call; though, come on, you—you know
you're treading serious ground, the minutes low
on your cell phone. No … Low is being wooed
like water by a stone—hours of whir
bending round conversation with a man
who's married, who's your friend, who, there, again,
tickles the boundary from straight line to curve
where silken, almost-not-there feelers fringe
the ground between the cloth of his marriage
and you, out here, wheeling newish luggage
around the weedy periphery … O, cringe
no more, you. You're just where you've always loved
to be—the lover, skirting love, but moved.

II

Gunfire in the woods—just rifles, just
deer. We wear orange vests when walking there
so no mistaking what we are. Discussed
my poem on the phone today, aware-
ness like a rain, that you've become the new
coarse knot my child-etched wood grain aims its flow
toward, dam-flown. Swallowing to join. That blue
starvation game. No oar. A man's rib bone.
At dinner, I told a poet, I'm scared I
think I might write for love. Seventy-one,
she smiled, said nothing, and then, *Well, why
not.* More was said. We're almost never done.
Outside, the world dilates, puts on its night,
and wonders what today we took for sight.

III

Today I took a walk to Fire Pond.
I brought the map, forgot the orange vest.
Into the silence I made human sounds,
coughs and heavy steps, proclaiming, *Yes
I'm here, but apart, I can't be folded
into whatever this is.* My steps pressed
words onto my mind: *Fire … Pond … Fire … Pond …*
which changed to my own name. I let the cadence
shield me. Early dark narrowed the spaces
between pines. Still I followed the map's lines
which trickled down toward that dark, labeled place,
an ink blot deep in the woods. But no sign
told what to do once there. *O*, it said to
no one. *Oh*, I echoed, embarrassed, new.

IV

Of course I want to send you these, how else
to know if they're good? Feels almost like be-
trayal, poems handled, cube by melt-
ing cube, to build a distance between me
and you ... Is that what I've been doing here?
Keeping something to myself, just to prove
I could? *I need to send out more this year,*
I said last time, responding to your drove
of acceptances. *What you need's to date
a poet,* you said, *a man who'll send out
for you.* Rather do it myself, I waited
to hear myself say, but suddenly found
it wasn't true. The first law of childhood
reclaimed its reins; I let it because I could.

V

This fire is the first I've ever built.
Outside: rain and gray. Thanksgiving's passed.
A man just left my room. Each second, *past*
relimns itself, takes one more log and wilts
away its frame. I'd think that I'd be through
deciphering another *You*. Look hard
enough into that center, it will shard
and burn. But *You* always returns as *Who*
then? just before the fire's died. So, off
I go again. I've noticed through the smoke
a little word that's pitched its tented hope
near every conflagration: *Yes … Enough*,
however, stays away. There's no such thing
when wanting is the hinge on which you swing.

VI

Okay. But what about when we make out
through screens of need and difficulty some
essence, faceless, still (the rain of doubt
sky-bound) behind another's eyes? I fum-
ble there, abashed. Or other times, I wait
for what will change: the shade redrawn, the light
put out. But sometimes—now—with you, up late,
I forget to think—don't want what might
be real, but *you*, in front of me—beside,
on top, below… And when you shook and groaned
I held you like an animal that's tied
and needs my help escaping rope and bone,
the grip of flesh. I held you while you died
and hoped when you awoke, we'd smile, confide.

VII

People are leaving every other day
it seems. No. Not leaving. Leaving *me*.
All the difference there: falling or be-
ing pushed. Old ache refinds me, in the way
aches do: a bloom inside the chest that hums
its hot fragrance to every sense, till noth-
ing isn't hunger. Nothing isn't loss.
The new *You*'s gone already too, the sum
of him dismantling, as time begins
to trickle, flow, between set features, drift-
ing landscape that was briefly home. The rift
of air, where something was, no longer is—
that is where we live, our true landscape.
And *now* is light condensed, a magic cape.

VIII

I leave here soon—a matter of days now—but
this place will keep on, without me. Others
will walk these paths, pine needles underfoot.
They'll look for Fire Pond and find it, hover
among the winter weeds or summer weeds
and feel the vulnerable indifference of
a place they've come to new, which hasn't need-
ed them so far, though they hope it will. Love
is similar. And so are other things.
From one hot lump, a thousand nerves that stand
on end like filings toward a magnet, sing,
at planetary pitch, of homesick, fanned
by ordinary wind—the world—its gall
for touching one, with gestures meant for all.

IX

Last night, your voice, resubmerged in New
York's held breath, sounded frozen as the Fire
Pond, which I visited today, a queue
of thoughts trailing. You said, *I'm only tired.*
But I saw through, my white-knuckle woods-vision
dissecting grays and browns with fearful glances
in order to discern the threat. My questions,
How *are* you ... *Sure* you're alright? were tense lances
cast at that moving target: your mood. I begged
most casually, in code, to know where you
had gone, what I could do to lift what sagged
between us. You contributed no clue,
said, *See you soon.* My stomach sick with failure,
some voice inside was steady: *Not another.*

X

So many strands. Can each be true? Must strum
them all at once. But chord implies a mood,
and mood's a screened-in porch, and watching from
there, only one view wears the tint of truth.
The trouble is that truth can overbear
what's true. Or what feels true: the constant reach
of detail's hands into the always-glare
of moment. Faces, phone calls, walks, the peach-
pit of fickleness that doesn't end
the world, or change it much, a willingness
to let the self loop out and back, to thread
each *You* anew, with special thread, a *Yes*
particular and voiced, but unbroken
from air—the blank thrum of need, awoken ...

III.

Woman drives past, crying

How can we trust ourselves
when one emotion, hot and bitter
as tea brewed long in the pot, pours
without permission into another day, which turns
into many days, until it cools
enough to feel almost comforting, until
you are sitting on a porch
one evening, mug pressed between your hands,
small lump of something like sugar
in your throat, and, squinting
into the distance (the only place
sunset or horizon can happen)
you look back at some loss
as an item on a list of things to do
turned up in the pocket of last year's coat,
and you think it touching in a way
when the sky quiets to ash, meaning
that it's time to go back inside
and tend to life—whatever that means
that particular night, when it seems
no one, anywhere, is suffering.

Infidelity

In my mind it's
    silent, colorless, violent
in its lurching grabs
    of motion, which is the only
kind of motion
    the mind can fathom,
unburdened by life's actual
    flow, which, by some dull
miracle, connects moment
    to moment to sound to thought
to weather to a nearly broken
    bedside table, as seamlessly
as the wet tissues
    of the body hold together
planes of existence
    that should never meet. Absurd
how effortless is the architecture
    of being. Intention, judgment,
forgiveness, these
    have no business being bound
in the same warm knot
    as those industrious veins
ushering blood to the gray in-roads
    of the brain. Nothing
is contained. No. Not true. If it were,
    conversation would have welled up
between them and the objects
    so perfectly near their bodies.
When moving from the porch
    to the bedroom

with wine-deepened lips,
        a breeze lifting the corners
of poems lying on my desk, why
        didn't he see? And why
did those words
        not seek out the warmest entry
to his mind? Why
        did my clothes hang quiet
in the closet, and never reach out
        their empty sleeves
to touch him?
        Then again,
perhaps he did feel them
        hanging there. And so the question
becomes not one of physicality
        or even lapse of memory, but a personal one
for him—of ethics I guess—something
        I am not able to connect
to that meeting (solid, undeniable
        as the black street below)
of his body with hers. A word
        like love, with its substance-
like confidence, has come unhinged
        from its shadow of meaning.
What if there never was a point
        of intersection, after all?
If they've only floated in each other's vicinity
        for convenience's sake, the way
a body suddenly feels more
        like an airplane seen from the ground
making its unswerving descent
        on aluminum wings
through incidental clouds.

First Flight

The man next to her wore a suit and a gold watch
which he often looked earnestly
in the face. He did not look her in the face.
Sometimes he pretended to look past her
out the window, but she felt his eyes
graze her body, as though it were the open field
below them, receiving the plane's shadow.

She was fifteen, and his look got inside her
like electricity, voices driven down
phone lines, clamoring over top
of each other, impossible to make out.
She wanted to cover herself, and also
to open her body completely to his eyes
where eyes had never been. She hated him, his

bovine calm, but also she felt
as she looked down at the green checkerboard
of farms, the river beaming into the distance,
the houses with their tiny roofs, fragile
as fingernails under the weight of so much
sky—she felt, as he stared at her, staring
at all of this, a power unfolding inside her chest.
Life had inched nearer like a warm body
when she wasn't looking, and suddenly—
she existed. Her confusion
was life's confusion.

Once, in the car with her mother, hurtling
through early morning fog, a deer appeared
at the edge of the white curtain the light hung
in front of them. She saw its eyes
shine, its muzzle twitch, the slender leg pause
mid-step. She had not been able to shut her eyes
or say a word. And then, like a secret, it dissolved
into the dark behind their car. Her mother changed

the radio to a country station, one hand
on the wheel, blue light on her face, not seeing a thing.

Elegy

(after Rilke's first *Duino Elegy*)

But the springtime refused me and went on living
      right up to the horizon of my skin, where
it paused, patiently rusting the parentheses
      that divided its meaning from mine—mine

an afterthought. What followed was accumulation
      of nights, one opening the next like the concentric
neck of a telescope, stretching its armored vision
      toward the sky—till one swampy July I found myself

in a cabin at the edge of woods, celebrating
      my birthday with a man who loved me, though
with difficulty, as I loved him. He was trying, I think,
      to drag a net up through our unfathomed

season, and retrieve only what was solid—
      summer's objects—sturdy, recognizable by
anyone with eyes. I wanted to be anyone
      with eyes, for a while—looking at fireflies, a lake,

some woods. We ate mussels, asparagus, crusty bread
      among dim lamps and candles, the expectation
that recasts the marrow of such places. I sensed
      we weren't alone, but lodged between ghosts—those past

vacation couples, who spoke smugly through the flowers
      stitched into the matching sofa and chairs, about
the tradition of love. We poured more champagne
      and moved to the porch. The dark was a unified mess

of cricket-rub and heat, condensed among the trees.
　　　　We were *surrounded*, but not *inside*. He held me
separate from the night. Our voices sounded extra, in-
　　　　essential, painted on dark water. How could we

compare? Our talk, our silence, our finite touch,
　　　　weren't dense enough to hold me in; I trickled out, awash
between him, the night, included in part, so excluded
　　　　in whole, panicked by the shortfall of the moment's

promise: my birthday, night away, a man whose everything
　　　　I hoarded. I had wanted to cross the distance
between us, as the crow flies: above the restless clock-
　　　　work rooms perform on our hearts, horizon a rush

of wind. I wanted it hard and soon, for years.
　　　　I barely had time to learn our customs—those
bright curtains, between which the world appeared
　　　　opaque, going on without us—

The End of Things

When I said what I felt
but didn't want to feel
the sky pressed down
our heads, bent and nodding
as two trees in adjacent yards.
The windows dulled
to glass in their panes. Above us
our children crawled back
from the edge of heaven
and melted into the public dark
all around us.

True North

Here at the edge of winter
      where the sky says *enough*
of all that, and begins to scrape
      our faces
of the inessential, lick tears into our lashes
      then freeze them—

where the wind is firmer
      than any voice, and strips
the pines, then dresses them
      in white—elderly
virgins, standing tall and straight
      in their nightgowns—

It's here I want to lay my body
      open to the ground, or melt
into the gray angles of some rock,
      to feel desire
loosen its attachment on any one
      object, to lose its focus

on *one*, and dissolve into its own
      expansion, a starker
passion, relieved to find nowhere
      a home.

Self-Preservation Ode

I've been trying all day to write an ode
to Spring—to its *fuck you*
froth of dogwood and crepe myrtle
quivering from a lip-raised snarl—
its cocky teenaged refusal to answer
the insipid red *Thank You*
the plastic bag offers, as it clutches
the edge of the creek—
its defiance of those
who would scold its green mind
and lack of guilt toward those who suffer
beneath its windy circus tent—

But how much of this is about the Spring?
All day I've been observing myself
trying not to observe myself
being weak—because screw
being weak, being
a tilled, fertile field, shrugging
its crops away. I want
to be the sun, preemptive and cruel,
scorching the fields to husk and ash
so the ground won't feel it
when the sky won't rain.

What I admire in Spring is its focus:
One needs a point to hone
to keep the peripheries at bay.
So I'll happily close down
those surrounding parklands
where friends and lovers pitch

their small tents, roughing it for a while
before they pack it up for home.
At night, flashlights bob and hold
inside the domes; they look, from a distance,
like paper lanterns, invisibly strung
on the wind. Still,
I'll be glad when they're gone.
Might as well be now.

Here, I *record* as the Spring records.
There will be no *This too shall pass*, no
cloistering of my throes behind stone
till they run clear of whatever bile
caused them. To *recognize*
really means to rethink
events, from a more reasonable
point of view (not mine). But
here, I *record* as the Spring records,
with attention to the details that matter
to Spring, blotting out whole histories
of hurt and wrongdoing, with impressions
of wind on a deep lake—

Epilogue

One last thing: I forgot to tell you

about the small gray mote
that rides the air before my eyes.

I don't remember the proper name
for such things; possibly I never knew.

But it swam, it rested, among the features
of your face; it was part of how I loved you

(I think). I see it now—that's certain—drifting
down the page. But these past years,

can I be sure? when no one moment
shoves forward from the crowd?

I can only know it was around the way
I guess the sun was too, proving each one

of our days to us. Isn't it enough
things disappear when we look away?

Pilgrim

I've been attended (in my efforts to fall in love
this month) by the mouse in my apartment, who's nested
its image everywhere: in a wadded receipt
beneath my bed, in the long-tailed phone charger, dying
beside its socket. It's hidden in the thistled ditch
my bed becomes when I sit up in the night, possessed
by a dream whose paws are still pressed to the smudged side
of my eyes, searching the sheets for what they see.

"*Something* ate that poison," I told you on the phone,
"It's got to materialize eventually." "Not necessarily,"
you said; and later, "Don't be afraid." *Afraid? Is that
what I am?* I was surprised. I imagined what would change
if you lived here too—how my private late-night vigils
would ungreen, snapped free of their source, collected
for kindling to make a fire in the clearing, and see
if there was enough to talk about (or do) till morning.

With you so far away, and us so new, it's been hard
to discern the likelihood of love. I've culled a nice image
of you as Pilgrim: earnest, straight-necked, boyish
New Englander—and found I was tickled by the thought
of your hard-working love, not yet called to its task—the city
still a wilderness, the hill stifling its light. I can see it
much better during the sprints my vision does
in the unmarked fields between our talks. But,

when you speak, each of your best qualities reveals itself
to be the uncomplicated twin of a subtler brother
you never knew, whose sense of irony, whose mind
like a sweep of moor, and eyes that aren't always averted

to the sky—never had the chance to rub off
on you. If one such brother had lived, I might tell him
on the phone tonight, how the mouse has finally arrived
dead at the foot of the stairs. How it was midday, not night,

when I found it. How it didn't seek a shoe or a pillow
or a kitchen drawer to die in, but curled up beside
the front door, as if wanting no more than to leave—
but how really the mouse lay down where it happened to be
when the poison sponged the last fluid from its body.
How its feet are tiny and simple at noon. How
my landlord will come in the morning and sweep
the bare gray fact onto the dustpan's gray-blue range.

Things said (me & others, dreams & waking, yesterday & years ago): An Exorcism

Red sky at night, sailors delight.

Tenure's a steep waterslide to death.

He's chairman of his own river, to be consulted before I drink.

It's your taste I can't stand, it's so bad.

Red sky at morning, sailors take warning.

If I were head-over-heels in love with you, time wouldn't matter.

You're like an evil superhero who uses her powers for good.

I feel like a vacuum cleaner that's never been cleaned.

There are worse things than being alone.

This headache is systemic.

Are there any spirits here who want to talk to us?

Whiskey's warming its hands at my soul.

If you see the whites of the leaves, rain is on the way.

Driving is an eye-contact sport.

What can I say? The Devil knows my name.

Every time a bell rings, an angel gets its wings.

Every morning I get on this bus all hard. Then I see you and go limp.

Attaboy, Clarence.

Please stop pursuing me.

Was anyone with you when you died?

No moon tonight. She's in my lap instead.

Since the moment you got here, you've been a terrible guest.

You are not your thoughts, you are much more than that.

If you conquer your subconscious mind, then you win the world.

What do you miss about being alive?
You're more a poem than a poet.
Your lips are soft as rose petals.
What about Platonic making out?
Your face looks blank.
You opened your eyes too soon.
I want to be anywhere but here.
How old were you when you died?
Could you be a ticking time-bomb and not know it?
What am I, chopped liver?
I knew there was something I liked about you.

Expression

Making love, for example. I've been trying
      to consider how that phrase implies artifice,
            production of something abstract, by means of physical

labor; but how, in Jane Austen's time, *making love* meant something
      like flirting on garden paths, or skipping promises
            deep into a reflected treeline. Yesterday,

Stephen's Lake never looked so made
      for nothing, the public trail circling it so paved
            against all possibility, as then, walking the long oval, balancing

abstruse monkey-bar thoughts
      toward a poem, which is really toward—what? Making something
            from another disappointment? Or, making fun, maybe,

of the guy who looked right at me, said,
      Let's make love
            right before we did, not two full morning hours

before he helped me toward the conclusion
      that this was only an expression—
            not of feeling

but of syllables,
      chosen for their flow, their gauzy, filmic effacement
            of all we didn't mean,

which courses now
      beneath the network of remembered events—
            watts of electricity, expressed

by the dull shock of streetlights, coming on
      one at a time. That's over now. An expression full of hubris,
            making love. I've hated it since I was fifteen and learning

how to park & execute
      lean five-point turns in the lot of Bushy Park,
            my old elementary school. As I made

one last slow round
      about the island of paltry shrubs & trees,
            my driving instructor leaned forward, lifted

his fat, wedding-banded hand
      from the smug perch of his knee, and said,
            There's two people *making love* in there.

His mouth sounded thick and full
      of satisfied knowledge, of mothballs that know
            all about the world of mothballs.

The windows of the white pick up we'd been circling
      were opaque. I craned my neck
            to check for oncoming obstacles

charging from the sidewalk or soccer field behind me.
      When a woman emerged, stepped
            down, lingering first, leaning back in, then glancing distantly

at us (one, now, inside our bright bulb
      of windshield),
            my instructor tried to hide his smile

behind his cluck of disapproval. *Marital affair,*
      he said, the words rolling sumptuously on his wetted tongue
            as he gazed out the window toward the woods

where decency still lay. Surely I *coloured involuntarily* then,
      as I did that morning with Make-Love the younger too
            (just dressed, frozen, overnight case dangling from my hand),

the way characters in *Pride and Prejudice* keep *colouring*
      these early autumn afternoons in my room, when
            what seemed the dignified property

of personal experience
      turns out to be public
            ground, muddied by impressions

others make and leave
      behind. There's shame, of course,
            in being trespassed, humiliation in standing still

at the center, a leaky fountain
      in the shape of a woman, giving itself away.
            Have I, then, abandoned myself

to motion, for vanity's sake? To take control, reinforce
      the perimeter, through sheer kinetic energy?
            It's true, even nothing

can inscribe its presence on the sky's
      thick mind, if it flees
            the swarming dark of stillness

and takes off, an icy draft of solar wind, kicking loose
      human signals, scripting cursive flares,
            forging bright blown glass

from formless sky. A universe of vanity
      in such comparisons. I wish sometimes
            I could quit talking, quit giving

it all away. Public displays of rejection
        and love never made should know better
                how to conceal pride's concealments, the center

from which the spokes escape; should know
        how to edit the limp from its tracks—unless, I
                suppose, the limp defines the style of the gait.

Brooklyn, February

Below this gritty sublet kitchen
cars unnerve the puddles'
light, the sky a lukewarm taupe
hosting two spires
from the church on Montrose.
Beyond, the flat hope
of windows, checkering a tall
apartment building. The walls
here are insulated
with noise—close-packed batting
of TV and voices, defining
where this room ends
and everything else begins—

Earlier, speeding under-
ground, each stranger seemed to be sinking
great volumes of energy
across that private event
horizon: the face.
It feels sometimes
like danger, this possibility
of being sucked like a room
through its own window—the fall
not a freedom, but a clawing
at condensation, a cawing
into a city with no buildings
to give back sound.

I miss lately the grounded feeling
of being *with* someone—the sense
that someone, always, is looking
even when no one is
in the room—I miss that knife-edge
verge of seizure
by another, every second
of the day, every second
the fear and joy of apprehension
by the eye's authority, threatening
to forever absolve me
of myself. *Grounded*,
meaning not being allowed
to float away or apart—being held
together and down.

The view from his bunk, lofted
and narrow, is a corner in Prospect Heights
where men yell, and strollers
clatter, attached to swaddled mothers
who race with bowed heads
to beat the yellow light. I ask
if he's ever seen the corner empty,
no movement.
I ask because I'm new
to the city, because he likes to think of me
as new. He doesn't know
I moved here because of him.
We argued earlier over drinks
because the play we saw was worse

than his plays, but more
successful. I tried to comfort him
which only made him angrier
since what he wanted
was to be angry.
We barely know each other.
Now he's climbing the ladder
into bed, wearing purple pants
and no shirt. We've no choice
but to lie very close.
We don't kiss, but squirm
against each other
as if trying to stay away.
Our hips move
the way wasps move, when pulsing
a threat with their stingers.
Our cheeks graze.
We're still pretending
we can't help it
right up until the end
when I'm looking down at a man
on the corner, both of us crying out.

Today I felt our passenger motion
as if from outside
the train, which nosed
into the dripping dark, over-
taking it, leaving it
behind. We were part of things, caught
in the narrow intimacy of that car, joined
to other cars, to the destination
and the people at the next station, facing the dark
tunnel, willing our train

to arrive. A feeling of pure
saturation: the this-ness
of moment, saturated
by the world, the world by us, us
by the world, all of it brimming
but stark, revolving, heartlessly
in motion. In heartless motion. A young couple
embracing; a nun folded
inside her body like bed sheets,
purple half-moons
beneath her eyes; the old feeling
that a glass thermometer is heating
my chest, its silver giving rise
to the red bulb
of anxiety, each time I face
the long commute to work
for S., who treats me
to miniature versions of myself—
each one a bit of lint, somersaulting
into corners, lacking
the gusto to fuse a whole
sweater, or some other
useful garment.

This flame pulsing from the candle
on the kitchen table, lives in what looks
like empty space, and looks
itself like matter. But it feasts
on invisible oxygen—touches
but cannot be touched.

Arrived at work early
(each train luxuriously
roomy, on time), my feet the first
to mark the new snow
tidying the back porch
of S.'s house. I unlocked
the door myself, entered
the basement office,
its two broad windows
eye level with the lawn
that slopes down to the white-cliffed
Hudson. A new brisk pride
in what wasn't mine
frisked the bruised peach
that had been leaking for months
in the closed paper bag
of my chest. But now I was someone
doing a job. I heard no movement
from the rest of the house
until one of the retrievers
came scuttling down the stairs
to lie at my feet and sigh his confidence
in the shared facts of our morning.

Reading through the *Emergency
Instructions*, affixed to a window
in the train, it admits
to three kinds: *Fire, Medical,* and *Police.*
For each, the first plea:
"Do not pull the Emergency Cord,"

followed by the rational
actions to take. Outside
the windows, black margins
show us thin pictures
of our faces. It may as well be water
out there, the tracks guiding us
through gritty, treacherous
depths. The sign warns, *Never exit*
the train, unless instructed to do so
by train crew or emergency
workers—people who work
an emergency, who grab
at the ribbons blowing wildly
from an invisible fan, who try
with gloved hands
to extract the wind
from disaster's manic furls.
Every so often
the walls outside flash with pictures
some teenager sprayed
in the cleared throat of the tunnel
before it screamed.

Fascicle

I come to your shores on a wave of disposable coffee cups.
        If you won't have me, I understand.
    It's Easter morning, and clear
I gave up nothing this season. A few specks of snow
            drift past the maple's red buds
whose birth and infancy you've remarked on
        from bed. I love that testament
to time's fruitful passage. Not for nothing,
            these late attempts. Never
    mind. The trail of coffee cups leads not
to consolation. But what about concentration
            on something that isn't you? I wish
to be that devoted scholar
        focused wholly on the perforations
        Dickinson's needle made
when she sewed folded sheets of paper into bundles
        of poems, dismantled after her death
            by a hand brutal in its lack
of clairvoyance; the scholar wholly focused
        on getting this crime undone—
            through his belief
in retrospect, in the tedious alignment
        of absences, slant similes
between the crested edges of pin holes
            that might string together
        a past. Not just a past. A way of seeing
down the impossible well
            into her mind, what she intended
to make her poems into. *To fill a Gap*
    Insert the Thing that caused it –

But if that cause is gone? Resurrect it, says the spirit
                        of the scholar.
You cannot solder an Abyss with air. Meanwhile,
        you. Burrowing deeper
into the space you've made, smiling
                        because we're at the diner
and I've just spilled ice water down my shirt
                        while trying to simulate
                spilling ice water down my shirt. If I'd practiced
giving something up this season, maybe
                        I wouldn't feel so attached
to the way you fill the space that will one day fill
                with something less fitting,
something that won't even pretend
                        to be you.
Is it a sin, or only a boring lack of faith
                to miss someone before they're gone,
to compulsively reassemble what has not yet
                        come apart? Your smile fossilizes
                in the wall of a duplicate diner
that has no walls; it will live longer
                        there. I'm laughing too, I'm there. Must not forget
that the needle, leaving its blank wake, is a point
                        of fact, not thought. You too
are light-sharpened and real. But I daydream
                all the time now, when you're not here.
Sometimes when you are. Sometimes I think
                I could stitch all the hours of my life
        into that element of blank
between facts and happenings, between trips
                        to the store, the bar, the library, Mass,
        if I went to Mass
anymore. I could stitch all my hours
                into the airy, unowned pools

that are the overflow, the glinting excess,
              of life's completed actions.
          Not isolated; connected
by being left behind, apart. I could give up
              everything, anything, a disposable coffee cup
traveling a current: filling, sinking, rising,
              emptying—Or else I could be
          like this plastic bottle of salty soda water
standing still in sunlight on the yellow table, trembling.
              No. I suppose that's being
          self-centered, and less
              like giving up everything
than nothing, more like sinking so far in
          to the leaden season of Lent, as to arrive
in its dark reversal, an overripe underworld
              of moveable feasts: Spring, broken into
through its absorbed, wall-eyed mirrors, then lived in
          for good, as happy ghosts who love love-
              making better, now
that nothing, not even their bodies, can come
          between them.

Notes

"Cogito": the title comes from Rene Descartes' famous dictum *Cogito Ergo Sum* or "I think, therefore I am." The italicized phrases in this poem were gleaned from John R. Cole's book *The Olympian Dreams and Youthful Rebellion of Rene Descartes* and Genevieve Rodis-Lewis's *Descartes: His Life and Thought*.

"Without": the epigraph is from Rilke's *Sonnets to Orpheus*, II, 13.

"Mirador": according to *Merriam-Webster's Collegiate Dictionary*, a mirador is "a turret, window, or balcony designed to command an extensive outlook." It stems from the Spanish/Catalan *mira(r)*, meaning "to look," and the Latin *mirari*, meaning "to wonder at." The italicized phrases in the poem come from Coleridge's letters, the *Biographia Literaria*, and from his poem "Dejection: An Ode."

"Fire Pond": Peterborough, New Hampshire, is the location of the MacDowell Colony, where I was a resident for two months.

"Things said (me & others, dreams & waking, yesterday & years ago): An Exorcism": two phrases in this poem are taken from the movie *It's a Wonderful Life*.

"Fascicle": the thread-bound bundles of poems that Emily Dickinson left behind are referred to as "fascicles," though the word is also used in anatomy and botany. R. W. Franklin is the scholar who tried to discern the original order and groupings of these bundles of poems by examining the pin holes in the paper left behind by Dickinson's sewing needle. The two italicized phrases in the poem are from Dickinson's poem 546, "To fill a Gap." Other images are taken from Dickinson's *Collected Poems*.

Acknowledgments

Grateful acknowledgment is made to the following journals, where these poems first appeared.

The Missouri Review: "Neighborhood," "Rotation"

Shenandoah: "Self-Preservation Ode"

North American Review: "Woman drives past, crying"

Michigan Quarterly Review: "Cogito"

Crab Orchard Review: "First Flight"

Many thanks to the Michener Center for Writers at the University of Texas at Austin, the University of Missouri's Creative Writing Program and Center for the Literary Arts, and the MacDowell Colony for their generous support of me and my poems. Special thanks to the following teachers, friends, and colleagues for their help with my poems, past and present: Mary Leister, Philip Singleton, Marie Howe, Naomi Shihab Nye, Khaled Mattawa, Susanna Childress, Carrie Fountain, Phil Pardi, Ibby Reilly, Scott Cairns, Lynne McMahon, Sherod Santos, Aliki Barnstone, Steve Gehrke, and David Wevill.

I also owe my deepest gratitude to my family—especially my parents, Mary and David Garratt, my sister Amanda, and my two grandmothers, Madeline McNamara and Virginia Garratt—who have supported me immeasurably over the years, in more ways than I can name. And to my wonderful and steadfast friends—thank you.

Finally, my heartfelt and humble thanks to Medbh McGuckian.